"God Isn't Done With Me Yet...."

Letters from the Street

Sr. Mary Rose McGeady

Covenant House

DEDICATED
to the
1,000,000
homeless children
who slept on America's streets last year,
scared, cold, hungry, alone,
and most of all,
desperate to find
someone who cares.

Table of Contents

Introduction

This is *Their* Story

They are like shadows in our cities and towns — small outlines of skin and bones that are visible against abandoned buildings, park benches, sidewalks. And these shadows disappear when darkness falls. Very few people know their faces, or their names. They are America's untouchables and unreachables — America's homeless street kids.

Who are these kids? How did they get there? Where did they come from? How do they manage to survive? Or do they....?

This is their story.

"God Isn't Done With Me Yet...." is my story about their struggle, written from my first-person vantage point as head of America's largest crisis shelter for kids. In this book I have written 21 separate monthly letters about these street kids — letters I wrote to friends and supporters telling them about these incredible kids who have passed through our doors and our lives.

These stories are unedited, stark, and sometimes graphic, mirroring the lives these homeless kids lead. Most important, these stories are *their* stories. Told by them. From mouths that quivered in fear, and in some wonderful moments, found the strength to smile and laugh.

I feel privileged God gave me the chance to be a part of it....

Sister Mary Rose McGeady
June 6, 1993

Chapter 1

*"I was afraid I was going
to die out there...."*

Lent, 1991

"A new mouth. If I could only have a new mouth, I think maybe it'd make me really happy."

She sat across the room looking so sad. The words came out slowly, haltingly, painfully, in a long continuous slur. I kept leaning forward, trying to catch the words, but it was really hard to understand her....

"I guess that sounds a little dumb, right? I know it must sound dumb to you. But my whole life ... ever since I was little ... my whole life I've felt like a freak. It really seems unfair ... it really seems...."

She looked up at me and let her eyes end the sentence. Her name was Alicia, a small girl with golden blond hair and blue eyes. If life were a little more fair, I think Alicia would've been sitting in a movie agent's office instead of mine. She really had beautiful features. She really could have been a beautiful girl....

Except one day, when Alicia was barely six months old, her "depressed" mother tried to kill her by feeding her a bottle of drain cleaner. Alicia somehow lived through the ordeal.

But her body was forever marked by the scars of

emergency surgery performed to save her life. Alicia was left with a deformed mouth. And a lifetime of pain.

"I know what you're thinking ... I'm lucky to be alive. I guess maybe you're right. But ... life's been really hard for me. Really hard....

"I never really had a home. I never knew my Dad. And my Mom ... well, after my accident she was so ashamed of me, she didn't want me anymore. I tried, but she didn't want me. So, one day when I was 15, I just left.

"I thought maybe life was getting better. I met a man, and I had a baby. She was so beautiful. I really loved her.

"But then my husband started beating me. I was so scared ... so messed up. I was afraid I might hurt my baby, I was so screwed up. So I gave her to an adoption agency and ran away. That was three years ago...."

Alicia ended up living on the streets, and selling her body, like a thousand other kids who've been hurt.

"I had to do it. I didn't know how else to get money. I was really taking a lot of drugs and drinking. Then I got scared. I was afraid I was going to die out there."

That's why she came to Covenant House late one night, hungry, strung out and crying.

"Can you help me?"

We couldn't wave a magic wand and make her scars vanish in an instant. We couldn't, overnight, calm the torrent of anguish and pain that coursed through her soul like an angry river. But we could pray with her and for her ... and we did.

We did pick up the phone and find a plastic surgeon. He specialized in cleft palate and "just happened" to be participating in the "Crippled Children's Fund" program.

He accepted Alicia as a patient. No charge.

Then a psychologist who donated one day a week to Covenant House agreed to meet regularly with Alicia.

Months later, Alicia stood in front of a mirror at Covenant House. She'd just come back from the plastic surgeon. He'd removed the last of her stitches.

Alicia's eyes sparkled as she was able, for the first time, to open her mouth wide.

She looked at herself in the mirror and kept opening her mouth and laughing and smiling and opening it again.

"Thank you, thank you so much. I've never felt this happy. Thank you, thank you." Her speech — for the first time — was clear. She couldn't stop saying thank you.

I'll never forget those last words she said that first bright morning she could speak. "Don't worry about me, anymore Sister," she said. "God isn't done with me yet."

The gates of heaven never saw a more beautiful smile....

P.S. As I finish this letter, the first day of Lent is upon us. I really can't say I enjoy Lent. I don't know many who do. It aches with so much sadness, human weakness, pain, loneliness, the death of things. I can't imagine that God expects our kids to understand, much less like, Lent either. For them, the penance and pain you and I practice during Lent is not limited to only one season, or one day: for them, their Lent is 365 days a year.

All I'm hoping for — all I'm praying for — is that you and I can help these kids understand that their long, lonely Lent can, and could, lead to something infinitely better: to a life without torment, and beatings, and spiritual hunger and dead-end streets. I know that might not sound like much consolation to a child on the street right now, but one day....

Your prayers for the kids this Lent would really be appreciated....

Chapter 2

"Every time they got drunk I got beaten...."

June, 1991

"I just want to sleep," he said.

"Please, let me sleep."

He stood outside our doorway, a little boy, propped on each side by two other homeless kids.

His left eye was so swollen and black and blue, he couldn't see a thing out of it.

His eyes dripped tears like faucets.

He was nine, maybe ten, years old.

For three days he wouldn't tell us who he was. "I just want to sleep," was all he said. "I just want to sleep."

We thought maybe he had been in a street fight. But after three days he finally began to trust us enough to tell us what had happened.

He had been beaten by both his parents at once.

Ten years old — one eye swollen — black and blue — cuts all over.

Andrew had run away from home.

"My mother and father ... they always beat me up," he finally told me. "Every time they got drunk, I got beaten up. I couldn't live there anymore, I just couldn't.

"So I ran away. I had to."

He was four foot six inches tall, with dirty brown hair and eyes to match, sixty-two pounds soaking wet ... and he was totally, completely alone.

"I was so scared after I ran ... I just didn't know what to do, Sister. I had some money I had saved up ... so I took a bus from my house on Long Island.

"I ended up just wandering around on the streets ... I didn't know where to go. Then I met those big kids who brought me here. They said maybe you could help me?"

Andrew stopped, and then looked up at me. I've never seen two lonelier eyes in my life. They lingered there for eight, ten seconds, getting heavier and heavier with each passing moment. It seemed like he was carrying the entire weight of the world in those eyes. Finally, though, it got to be too much. The floodgates began to open. Andrew just put his head down, and cried.

I had to take a quiet deep breath or I would have started crying, too.

"I'm so sorry Andrew. I know how hurt you must be ... how painful it must be. We all feel so lucky you found us ... we're really glad you came to us."

"Those big kids were right, Andrew. We do want to help you.

We really want to help you. Will you let us?"

He looked up at me, biting his lip as hard as he

could, trying to stop the tears for a minute. Then, his head started bobbing up and down, first slowly, then faster and faster. I could tell he really liked the idea a lot.

"Okay, Sister," he finally said. "Okay."

"Thanks Andrew," I said and I gave him a big hug. "Thanks for letting us be your friend."

This entire conversation took place about three and a half hours ago. As I write you this letter, I have no idea what's going to happen, long-term, to this beautiful — and very courageous! — little boy.

I wish I had a better answer than that. But right now I don't.

I feel very strongly that Andrew should not go back to his parents unless they get professional help. No way! This little boy should not suffer this way ever again.

As for what will happen to Andrew while he is with us, I can tell you this. We will love him and care for him. Every moment he is at Covenant House, he will know from us that he is special, and worthy, and loved.

Every single child — every child! — deserves to know that he or she is loved.

Andrew has probably never known that feeling.

But he will. I promise you he will.

Please, do you think you could say a prayer for him tonight, and all the rest of our kids? Your prayers would really mean a lot to me and Andrew right now. (They've already meant so much, so many times before.) Please.

> We never, ever stop praying for you.
> He is, after all, just an innocent child....

Chapter 3

"I'm glad the pimps don't like us...."

July, 1991

"Help! Help me! Please help me!"

She came sprinting out of the darkness, as fast as her legs could carry her, and literally jumped on the running board of our van.

She kept banging on the window — pounding, pounding — to get our attention. Her eyes were overflowing with fear.

For a split second, we were scared to death she'd fall off and kill herself.

Our driver slammed on the brakes, and grabbed for the door to let her in.

"No, no please don't stop here. My man is watching ... he'll see me get in. He'll know where I am. Go over to that alleyway over there. I'll get in then when he can't see me. He'll never know where I went...."

Before we could convince her to jump in, she leapt off the van, and raced off to a different alleyway. She was running, swerving, dodging across the dark street, doing all she could to confuse whoever it was — whatever it was — that was chasing her.

We stepped on the gas, and raced our van to the alleyway she had asked us to go to. Our driver turned off the van and the headlights, and waited in the darkness.

Seconds later, the girl came running toward the van, from another direction. In an effort to fool her pimp, she had run completely around the block.

She was only about 30 yards from our van and safety. Then it happened.

A huge car came screeching around the corner, its headlights off in the darkness, and aimed itself directly at our van.

Sheila, our van driver, spotted the car at the last minute, turned the key, and slammed on the gas. The car barely missed ramming our van.

Then it sped off, and headed right for the girl.

Although it was impossible to really see much in the darkness of midnight, it was clear that the girl was very, very young. Fifteen at the most, maybe even twelve or thirteen.

She raced across the street, with the car right behind her. The car careened over the median strip, over curbs, like a hungry shark after its prey.

Finally, it pulled alongside the girl. A man jumped out, grabbed the child by the throat, and started beating her.

And then he picked her up, and threw her into the car.

Our van raced after the car as fast as we could. Sheila took the license plate number, and telephoned it into the police.

But they said there was nothing we could do.

The car got away. Our van hasn't seen the girl for a week. We're really worried if we'll ever see her again.

I wish I could tell you that this was some sickening scene I saw from some Grade-B movie, filled with make-believe actors on a make-believe streetcorner.

But I can't. *Every single word of this story is true!*

I can't get this girl out of my mind. I keep thinking about her every minute. She was so close to my outstretched hands, so close to being saved. But she ended up in the scummy hands of her pimp, a sick man driving a big car, sleazing through life at the expense of little girls.

I hope you'll excuse the brutality of my letter this month. This is not the letter I had planned to write!

I was going to write you about a beautiful 16-year-old girl named Donna, one of our newest walking, talking, smiling success stories. I walked on air for two whole days after I met Donna, her story was so beautiful. I really wanted to tell you about her this month.

But then I met this girl running toward our van. I can't get her out of my mind. I just had to tell you about her.

I'm having a little trouble finding the words I need to say. I guess I feel the need to stress something I'm sure you know already. Covenant House is not "make-believe." Not every ending is a "happy ending" for our kids.

In trying and crying and sweating to save the lives of homeless kids, we don't always succeed.

I think if I had to really sum up what we are, we're just a good shelter for kids that is deliberately placed in the midst of a sometimes horrible, dangerous world ... right where God wants us to be.

Our volunteers and staff — wonderful people like Sheila driving the van — put themselves at risk every day. (Not long ago, the back window of our van was shattered by gunfire.)

A pimp — angry because we were trying to "steal" one of his girls — shot at our van. Other pimps have thrown rocks at us, knives at us ... everything.

But do you know what? I'm proud the pimps don't like us. Because none of us here care much for them either. I don't like them. And I'm going to keep making sure we do everything in our power to stop them.

We're never going to turn our backs on these lost children.

Chapter 4

"I've made this promise to God...."

August, 1991

NUN FOR HIRE

Catholic nun looking for a chance to speak at churches and civic groups about God's kids. Great stories of kids in seemingly hopeless situations, desperate escapes, daring rescues, heartwarming love, happy endings.

No salary requested! (But I would like the chance to ask for donations to help homeless kids!)

If interested, write to: Sister Mary Rose, Covenant House, 346 West 17th Street, New York 10011. An Equal Denominational Speaker.

Do you belong to a church group that might be willing to listen to this nun for a few minutes? Maybe a PTA? I'd love the chance to tell you about our beautiful kids. I've got some really incredible, heartwarming stories to share. (You'd be surprised how many kids come from your neck of the woods!)

Please let me know, if you can. I've made a promise to God that I'm going to talk to anyone and everyone who'll listen, to tell them about our homeless kids ... and beg for their help.

Ever since God put me in this new position as President of Covenant House (I'm convinced he arranged the whole thing), I've been looking for ways to get the word out about our kids.

Give me a call. I've got some really great things to tell your friends.

Chapter 5

*"For a long time I thought that's
what love was.*

*Finally, I just couldn't
take it anymore...."*

September, 1991

"It started one night with my older brother Dan....

"One night he just came into my bed, and he ... he did things to me.

"I was so scared, Sister ... I didn't know what to do.

"Then a couple days later, he brought my older brother Kevin in with him.

"And then another night ... another night my father came in too.

"I was eight years old, Sister...."

After you've worked with homeless kids as long as I have, you begin to think you've heard it all. But then you meet someone like Colleen.

Just five minutes earlier Colleen had looked like any happy-go-lucky 17-year-old girl. I had noticed her right away, standing in our Crisis Center, smiling and laughing, her thick auburn hair bouncing, and freckles dancing around her pretty nose.

But then I went up to her and asked her how she ended up at Covenant House. That's when the smile got harder and harder to see, and the freckles stopped dancing. That's when she started to tell me how a pretty girl with freckles ends up homeless on a city street.

"This went on for four years, Sister.

"When my brothers and my father did things to me, they would say, 'Colleen, you're such a love. I love you.'

"For a long time I thought that's what love was.

"Finally, I just couldn't take it anymore. I knew everything was wrong. I told my mother and she got mad at me. She didn't believe me about my brothers. But that night I heard her ask my father.

"And he just said, *'Yeah. So what? She's not my kid.'*

"That was how I found out that my father wasn't my real father."

Colleen paused for a long minute and stared off into the corner, to some place very, very far away. I wanted to just stop and throw my arms around her, but I could sense she wasn't ready for that yet.

Colleen wanted to tell me more. She had to.

"By the time I was 11 or 12, my mother and my stepfather had five younger kids, and my mother made me drop out of school to take care of them. I just hated it, Sister ... I was so mad.

"When I was 14 I couldn't take it anymore and I ran away, and stayed at a friend's house. I told her mother what was going on and she called the police. The police wanted me to press charges, but I was scared that everyone would hate me so I didn't. In fact, I went back home.

"I still don't know why. I guess I didn't know what else to do.

"I worked almost all the time, at a pizza place. But my mother took all my money and when I wasn't working I had to watch the kids.

"Finally, I just left for good and I ended up on the streets. I can't tell you how bad that was, Sister. It was ... it was...."

Colleen dropped her eyes to the floor, and lifted up her hands to stop the tears.

I thought about saying something about how bad I felt and how much I loved her, and how much I understood ... but I realized that this wasn't one of those times when words would help much. Colleen had heard enough words in her life.

I reached out and hugged her. She stood there and sobbed in my arms.

I wish I could tell you that Colleen's story of unending abuse by her own family is unusual. But it isn't. We hear it — we see how it ravages a kid — all too often at Covenant House.

I wish to God I understood it all better.

I guess after 40 years working with troubled kids you might think I'd have some special answers — some intuition — into why a parent sexually abuses an innocent child. I wish to God I did have those answers.

I think you'd be utterly amazed if you knew the extent of incest on our society. As hush-hush as it is, it is more prevalent than you can imagine.

I ask myself — how can someone violate that incredible trust between parent and child ... and then ruthlessly abuse innocence.

I do know that we will do all we can, everything we can, to help Colleen and all the others somehow work through the pain in their lives. At the very least, we want to make sure that Colleen understands that she is loved here the way children are meant to be loved. With respect. And warmth. And dignity. And trust. And compassion.

And most of all, with no strings attached. That's what the Covenant we have here is all about.

And we also want her to know that God loves her, too. That's so incredibly important! We need kids like Colleen to know that God will never forget her.

He expects us to do everything we can to be his love for her now.

Please ... do you think maybe you could help again this month? I know it's a lot to ask (you've been so generous so many times before), but will you help us do everything we can for Colleen and all our other kids?

There are so many kids like Colleen here who desperately need all the love you have to give. Some of them are new kids who just came to Covenant House for the first time tonight, totally lost, completely unprepared to open up yet and trust us.

And a lot of them are like Colleen, kids who are finally coming to grips with their pain, quietly crying to a counselor, secretly praying that maybe a bright new life will finally begin for them.

The hundreds of kids we'll see this month are all so different, kids with different problems, at so many different stages in their lives. But all of them have one very important thing in common. They need — each and every one of them — food and clothing, shelter and medicine, and counseling and love just to survive another day.

And if we're not here for them — if Covenant House is not here to hold Colleen in our arms — then no one will help them. Our kids need us that much.

They need you that much.

I consider it such a special privilege that God has placed me here to help Colleen and the others. These kids are so very, very beautiful!

Chapter 6

"I guess this is TV virginity week."

October, 1991

Doogie Howser has decided he's going to have sex with his girlfriend this year. After all, he's 18, and don't all 18-year-olds "do it?"

Terry, a teenager on the TV show "True Colors," is getting ready to "become a man," too. During this season's premier episode, his TV family spent much of the program ridiculing Terry for being a virgin. His non-virgin girlfriend has made it clear she'll help Terry with his problem....

And on PBS TV's "In the Shadow of Love: A Teen AIDS Story," a high school senior engages in unsafe sex while "researching" a report on AIDS. ABC Television broadcast the same program as an "Afterschool Special."

And the examples go on, and on, and on.

As you read this letter, you and I and the rest of the American public (and yes, its children) are being fed an unprecedented orgy of random sexual activity by teenagers on our television screens.

In fact, to quote a widely-distributed story published in the *Los Angeles Times* ... teenage sex in the opening week of the just-begun television season *"was happening all over the dial. I guess this is TV virginity week."*

I wish just once one of these TV producers would take a walk through our crisis shelter.

Then I'd introduce him to the kids who don't appear in their 30-minute sitcoms. Real kids in really tough situations. I'd ask them to talk to Lureen....

Lureen is a tiny 13-year-old kid who has a pony tail, and a nice smile, and something else — a little baby named Tony. "He's going to have everything I never had, Sister. Everything...." Lureen is also homeless.

And perhaps those same producers would like to meet Melissa. Melissa knocked on our crisis shelter door last week, holding a beautiful baby boy named James in her arms. She's going to live at our Mother/Child Center because she has no where else to live. Melissa will turn 17 next week.

And then there's Wendy. Wendy's a wonderful, wonderful child, who's suffered through more pain in her lifetime than any child should ever have to bear. Her father left her. Her drug-addicted mother abused her. "I thought maybe having a baby would make things better," Wendy told me. "But you know what, Sister? I love my baby, but I don't know how to care for him. I mean, I need a job, I need money. I'm really scared right now."

And then there are Joanne, and Ginny, and Betty, and Katrina. And so many others. All very beautiful and well-meaning children, holding children of their own. They are going to need all the help and the prayers we can give them.

Listen, I'm praying I don't sound like some raving expert who thinks she has all the answers about a very complicated and disturbing national issue. There are lots of reasons why kids who have no reason to even think about adult-type relationships, start them. There are tons of sociological reasons why 2,795 teenage girls will become pregnant today, and another 1,295 teenage girls will give birth. TV isn't all to blame, not by a long shot.

And I am second to no one in my belief that freedom of expression is a precious right that no one, but no one, should ever take away from us. But I believe very strongly that television should be responsible ... be a positive force in our children's lives.

But that's just the point. Who is watching these shows?

It's not just adults, it's children. Children too young to know that just because something is shown, it's not necessarily correct. Children like Lureen and Melissa and Wendy who will spend the rest of their lives trying somehow to raise a child ... and who will never, never recover from the fact that they were too young for parenthood.

What advice will America's "shapers of young minds" in Hollywood give our kids? How will they neatly provide a happy ending for our kids, tied up in the 29th minute with a few laughs and a big hug? Do they know our kids are here ... sitting in a crisis shelter, cradling an infant? Do they care?

For anyone to blithely proclaim that what Hollywood shows on TV doesn't affect our children, and their values, and how they think about the incredible responsibility of caring for another life ... that's simply wrong.

And you and I are left to pick up the pieces, as best we can. It just isn't right. It just isn't right....

Earlier tonight, I walked down to our crisis shelter where about 15 kids — homeless, young, older, black, white, boy and girl — were huddled around a television set.

These tough, street-hardened kids were reacting to a TV show they had chosen, all by themselves, on their own. A show called "Little House on the Prairie." A show about family. And values. And caring.

It's the kind of show our kids wanted to see tonight. Maybe because it showed them all a life they have never known. Maybe there's a message in there....

I know this letter is a lot different than the ones I usually send you. I guess it was seeing Lureen, and Melissa, and Wendy all about to climb a mountain called life, holding little babies in their arms. And then I saw this article.

Please, do you think you could think of my kids and their kids tonight? The ones dealing with a real-life struggle to raise a child? The ones who simply won't make it unless you and I reach out to them and help.

And, please talk to your kids about what they're seeing on television. Don't be afraid to talk to them about values ... tell them what you truly believe.

Chapter 7

*"The repetition of the
original Christmas scene."*

Christmas, 1991

My dream of a perfect Christmas is to wake up and find Covenant House empty.

I mean, I wish just once I could walk down to our crisis shelter on Christmas Eve, and tell our kids they won't be needing us this Christmas. "I just got off the phone," I'd tell each and every kid. "I just talked to your family," I'd tell them. "They said they miss you ... they love you ... and they want you to come home."

And then I wish they'd all file out the door, one by one, smiles on every face, and say good-bye. "I gotta go now," they'd all tell me. "I'm going home," they'd all say. "I hope you have a nice Christmas too, Sister. Take care, I probably won't be seeing you again...."

No homeless kid would knock on our door that Christmas day. No child would be hungry. No boy or girl would walk the streets, desperate and alone, with no place to go.

I wish ... I wish ... I wish....

I think I love Christmas as much as anyone in the world, but it's pretty hard to handle at Covenant House

— for us and the kids. Yes, there are lots of presents and a good meal, and the kids try their best to be happy (I think they try really hard at appearing happy because they know that's what we want for them).

But amidst all the smiles and hugs, I can't help but feel very sad for our kids too — especially the ones who show up for the first time on Christmas day, the newest homeless kids, the ones who seem the most vulnerable and sad and afraid.

"I never had a good Christmas, Sister," a sad boy named Mattie told me last Christmas morning. "I never remember getting a Christmas present ... eating a Christmas dinner ... feeling like a happy family," he told me. "My parents used to lock me in a closet ... they didn't want to bother with me."

I wonder how it feels to be that unloved on Christmas day? To be alone? To be a child and spend Christmas day locked in a closet, or alone on a street...?

In a few days, as we celebrate Christmas once again, we will pause and pray to remember a baby who was born into a cold, harsh world, without a home to take comfort in. And even when He grew up, the world wasn't ready to accept Him, much less love Him.

I think this Christmas story belongs to our kids, in ways a lot of them may never fully understand. Many of them have been born into a cold, cruel world, and with a lot of people who aren't ready to accept them, aren't willing to support them, aren't willing to give them the love and the help they need.

And like the Christ Child before them, these kids desperately need someone to watch over them and care about them. To love them....

I mean, the Christ Child was not all by Himself. If almost 2,000 years ago in a cave in Bethlehem it was just the baby lying down there in a crib with no family, no human comfort and no one to watch over Him, it wouldn't have been nearly as comforting a sight, would it?

But when we see the Christ Child surrounded by love, by Mary and Joseph, and the shepherds, the wise men, the togetherness and the faith that comes with family — I think that's what makes the scene so beautiful.

So it is with *you*, too. *You* are what makes *our* Christmas story beautiful. Every time you stand beside our workers, and our volunteers, you surround our children with family — with love. Your prayers and support are like the gifts the wisemen placed before the Christ Child.

When you really stop to think about it, our house is a manger to these kids. Our vision of faith at Covenant House really is this — that we see in every youngster the repetition of the original Christmas.

So this year, as you and I pause to give thanks, I pray you will join me in asking our Lord to send our kids someone in their lives who will help them feel worthwhile and loved and cared for. Because I think that's what makes the difference. Only when we experience that kind of love can we share in the reality of love, which is God.

That's the Christmas I wish for our kids....

My dream of an empty Covenant House? Well, it won't happen this year. In fact, Covenant House will be a mob scene on Christmas Day. Kids we haven't seen in years, new kids we've never seen, kids who come off and on— they'll all come to us on Christmas because they desperately, achingly need someone to care about them.

The best I can truly hope is to recreate the love of the nativity for every child who comes to us.

The most I can hope for is that you too, will help us bring that beauty to them. We can't do it without you.

Chapter 8

"I don't have anyone...."

January, 1992

"He called me a freak," she said.

"I'm ... I'm tired of everyone telling me I'm a freak."

I moved a step toward her, and tried to put my arm around her, but I was too late. Her body crumpled like dead weight to the floor. She kept burrowing her forehead against the carpet, trying to hide, trying to avoid looking at me. She was crying her eyes out. It was 7:30 at night, two days before Christmas....

I began to comfort her, but she stopped me before I could get the words out. "I know what you're going to say, Sister. But don't, okay. I'm an ugly freak, and everyone knows it.

"I mean, does this look normal to you?"

At that moment, she lifted up her right hand, and flashed it before my face. "Does it?"

I took her hand in mine before she could pull it away. Huge scars ran all across her hand, on both sides. I don't ever remember seeing a hand more badly burned and disfigured.

Her name was Sharon. She was only 16.

Fifteen years ago, when Sharon was barely a year old, her mother had put her baby's hand over a burning gas flame "to teach her a lesson." For second after second, Sharon cried out in incredible pain, but her mother held the hand still. Doctors did all they could to help her, but there really wasn't a lot they could do.

The scars, inside and out, became permanent. Since that moment, Sharon has been ridiculed and laughed at by kids wherever she's gone. Even today, most kids only know her by her nickname, "Freddie Krueger," after the deranged and deformed character in those awful "Nightmare on Elm Street" movies.

God knows Sharon could have probably overcome this intense hurt with the love and support of people who cared about her. But no one ever has. Sharon never had a mother again — authorities took her away. For 15 years now, she's spent her life being shuffled from one foster home to another to another, never once finding a loving parent who would give her the love and support every child needs.

Not too long ago, we found her for the first time — sleeping in a corner, under some newspaper, at the Port Authority Bus Station.

"I don't have anyone," she said when she first walked through our doors. "I don't have anyone...."

I talked with Sharon for a long time about the pain and hurt she felt. It became obvious that she was crying less about her hand than her heart.

I talked a little too about how God loves her, and how she is a very special creation of His love.

It really hurt to talk to her. She is such a great kid. But she thinks she's ugly because when she looks in the mirror she sees what everyone reminds her of every day: a disfigured hand, and a lifetime of pain.

She's not yet ready to see what you and I see in her — a child of God ready to blossom, if someone just gives her the chance.

By the time you get this letter it will probably already be a new year. On behalf of all our kids, I want to wish a very happy New Year to you and those you love. Thank you for seeing the infinite beauty of kids like Sharon. Thank you for seeing beyond their scars and bruises, which they carry like crosses through their lives. Thank you for loving them when many others don't.

And, we hope — we pray every day — that you'll keep our kids in your heart this coming year. This cold weather is a real killer for us. More kids — more desperate kids — come to us right now than any other time all year.

We could really use your help right now. The need is very, very urgent....

Chapter 9

"Who else is going to help them?"

February, 1992

I kind of wish God would write this letter for me.

I mean, I've got some very important things to tell you this month. And I'd love to see what He would write you — I'd love to know what He would say.

"I need you to read this, my friend," His letter might say. "It's about some of my favorite kids in the whole world. I think you're one person who would want to hear this," His letter would go on.

And when you were done reading His letter, you would know and feel and see *everything* He wants you to know and feel and see about our homeless kids. And none of our kids would ever want again, because you would share His letter with your friends. Millions of people would suddenly discover our kids for the first time and love them and care for them as much as you always have.

I really wish He would write this letter for me....

God knows we need a little extra help from Him right now. To be blunt, we're having a lot of trouble making ends meet at Covenant House these days (maybe He would say it that directly, too?)

We're used to dealing with a lot of rough times and ups and downs — we've been doing that, with God's help — for 23 years. But in all our 23 years, we've never had to deal with a recession like the one that's beating us now. And it's really hurting us!

The fact is, the recession really cut into Christmas giving to Covenant House this year.

A lot of friends just weren't able to help as much as they did in the past. Donations to Covenant House — and other good charities, too — were a lot lower than even our lowest estimates.

And to make matters worse, this is all happening in the middle of the winter.

Winter's our toughest time around here. By far. Take sheltering our kids, for example....

Kids on the street desperately depend on us to help shelter them (who else is going to help them?) And it's so hard keeping a warm roof over their heads right now. I'm sure I don't have to tell you how much more expensive it is to heat your house in the winter. You can imagine heating our home, and providing hot showers for hundreds of shivering boys and girls! The cost is really astounding.

But that's just the beginning....

Then there's the matter of feeding kids this time of year. I don't know if anyone's ever done a formal study on this, but I can tell you from experience — the colder it gets outside, the more kids eat. A homeless kid can burn up hundreds of calories a day just standing outside in the cold. You'd be amazed how much extra food our kids need when they come in from the cold.

And then ... throw on top of all that the extra clothes these kids need, all the extra medicine we go through this time of year, and on and on and on.

I hope I don't sound like I'm complaining. I thank God every day we are jammed to the rafters! If these kids didn't find us, they'd be out on the freezing streets alone.

But these costs are overwhelming us right now. I keep trying to stretch our budget a million ways, but it's past the point of stretching any farther.

I'm worried and scared.

We've made a Covenant with these kids — to protect them and love them — and we're just not going to break it. I simply won't. And I know you don't want to break it either. It wouldn't be a Covenant if we did that....

That's why I'm writing you this letter. I'm wondering if there's any way you could help our kids by making a special big donation today. I don't know any other way to say it. I need your help right now.

I know this is a lot to ask of a friend, especially someone who's been so generous. But my back's against the wall now.

Do you think you could help? Please.

Believe me, any donation you can make now will make a difference. It will be one of the most important you have ever sent to help our kids.

And even if you can't help (and I'm praying you

can!), I really hope you can say an extra prayer for our kids right now. The Covenant you and I have made with these kids is the best thing — in many cases, the only good thing — in their lives.

Please, could you do that, and help them too, if you can?

Thanks so much for reading this letter. May God bless you with a blessed and joyous New Year.

P.S. I meant what I said at the beginning of this letter — I really wonder what God would say to you and me if He were in my shoes writing this note. I think maybe He would have spent the entire letter writing about the Covenant we have rather than writing about recession, and heating bills, and runny noses. I really don't know why God has asked His kids to walk the difficult path they do. I wish I understood all that better. But I think He might even say He's got an extra soft spot in His heart for our kids. But I'm sure He'd spend a lot of time reminding us how much He loves the kids; and how they are all His.

Chapter 10

"I just found out something bad,"
she said. "I'm HIV positive."

Lent, 1992

The sweet smell of chocolate chip cookies steam-rolled through the cafeteria and stopped at my nose. I stared down at my nose, and urged it not to notice. It was 1:30 in the afternoon, Ash Wednesday, and I'd already promised God that sweets (among other things), were on Sister Mary Rose's "1992-give-up-for-Lent" list.

"This batch sure does smell good, doesn't it Sister?" smiled Horace, one of our Rights of Passage kids training to be a cook. "You really know how to hurt a nun," I smiled back. The bedlam of 50 hungry kids eating and joking drowned out our laughter.

The Covenant House cafeteria is one of the greatest places here on earth, I think. Every day, six times a day (the kids eat in shifts because there are so many of them), 200–300 hungry kids file through its doors, and find a piece of home they never had.

Filling empty stomachs is probably the least of it! Here, amidst 10 round tables, a homeless kid gets to feel what it's like to be cared for. And watched over.

And cared about. Often for the first time.

I was standing there, drinking in the bedlam, when I suddenly felt a tug at my sleeve....

"Excuse me, Sister," she said. "I got to talk to you," she said. "I got some really terrible news."

I grabbed Donna's hand and eased her over to a corner, where we could be by ourselves. Her eyes really had me worried. They were very, very scared.

"I just found out something bad," she said. "I'm HIV positive," she said. "No one else knows it."

"I mean, just look at me Sister," she said. "I'm getting skinnier every day." She looked up at me, and the tears started gushing out faster. "Don't cry, Mommy," her beautiful two-year-old baby said. "Don't cry...."

I reached out to Donna and hugged her and the baby as hard as I could. "Maybe the HIV isn't the reason you've lost weight," I said. "You might not have AIDS, yet," I said. "We're all hoping that they'll come up with something to help people with HIV," I said.

She reached out to me, and hugged me again. "I hope you're right, Sister," she said. "I hope you're right."

"At least my baby's all right," she said. "I got her tested too, Sister," she said. "She's negative, thank God."

I suddenly felt like crying too. I mean, I love all our kids, but Donna is one of my favorites. Ever since she was 15 (she's 18 now), Donna has been without a family. Donna's never had a father, and she was abandoned one night by her mother who's a drug addict.

For two long years she roamed the streets, without friends, without family, doing things she didn't want to do but had to, just to eat and survive. Then she found Covenant House, and hope. And a mission in life. "I want to work with retarded kids," she told me last year. "I'm going to school to help retarded babies. These kids need my help," she said.

And she did. For the past eight months, she's worked with retarded children. This girl who has every reason to hate this world, somehow found the strength to try to help its most needy. Donna really is a beautiful kid.

Now she's HIV positive.

"I think you should know something right off, Donna," I told her. "HIV isn't going to change the way I feel about you, or the way Covenant House feels about you," I said.

"We're going to keep loving you, and helping you learn how to love your baby, and take care of special kids. You don't have to be afraid to tell people here about your illness," I said. "Everyone here is just going to love you a little more."

I think maybe God sent Donna to me, on Ash Wednesday, for a reason. I mean, Lent is all about reckoning, and tough questions, and looking in the mirror and seeing if we like what's staring back at us. (Lent is very good for us I think, even if it is really hard sometimes....)

It's a time to reflect on how we use the goods of

this world, and how we deal with our relationships. It's a time to ask ourselves whether we're really living a life of love, or just going through the motions. It's a time for taking a long hard look at our souls and seeing where the defects are. It's a time to make resolutions to turn our life around, and then begin the painful process of doing just that.

It's not easy spending 40 days staring in to the mirror of our soul, scrutinizing, writing checklists, grading our own performance. But it's good for us, I think....

Our kids? Kids like Donna? They're not as lucky as you and me. Our kids live in a perpetual Lent ... an eternal blur of painful reckoning, questioning, excruciating self-examination.

I mean, you and I may "give up things" these next 40 days by choice. Our kids have spent an entire lifetime "giving up" things ... things that no kid should ever be forced to give up.

They "give up" home because they have been beaten and abused so much they simply can't live there anymore. In running to the streets, they "give up" all hope of being loved. They "give up" all hope of being cared for. Or nurtured.

When you talk to kids like Donna there's an unmistakable element of dying in our kids' lives — full of remorse — tinged with self-blame. Did I make the right choice in running away? Why doesn't anyone love me? Is it my fault? Why?

Lent is in their hearts every minute of their lives....

And we love kid's like Donna as much as we can,

as long as we can. Without fear or judgement. Without reservation or restraint. Unconditionally, totally, always.

P.S. I know that God has a very special place in His infinite heart for Donna — I absolutely, positively know that. I'm sure — positively sure — He understands better than I ever could her deepening loneliness, her anxiety becoming fear becoming terror, her despair over the unknown fate that awaits her. The aloneness and fear and terror and abandonment all our kids feel ... they share that with Him in a very unique way.

Chapter 11

"I'd be lost without this house...."

March, 1992

He swooped in on me about five seconds after I had sat down in the chapel.

"Hi, my name is Terry," he said. "Would you mind if I sit next to you," he asked.

"I'd like that," I said.

"Great," he said.

He had a sweet face, big blue eyes, and a white T-shirt that made him look like the "all-American boy." And he couldn't keep still. Every time I took a breath, Terry was jumping out of his chair, greeting kids who walked through the door. He had to be real quick on his feet. Within five minutes, all thirty chairs were filled.

"It's time to start, Sister," he said. "I think you'll like this," he said.

Up front, behind the altar table, a young boy named Robert began to lead the room full of homeless kids in prayer. He asked God not to remember the past, but only to look at the present. He asked God to see the good resolutions that filled every heart in the room. He begged God for strength, and courage, and hope.

Then he opened the floor up for prayers....

"Help my father to understand me," a young boy said. "Make it happen that one day we can talk to each other."

"God, help me get a good job," another boy said, "and help me keep it when I get it."

"Thank you God, for giving me the strength to walk away from drugs," a girl said. "And please God, give me the strength to stay straight."

On and on the prayers went, each kid praying from the heart. In the middle of one prayer, as my hand rested on the arm of my chair, Terry's hand came over and he placed it on top of mine very quietly. He looked at me, and I looked at him, but we didn't say anything.

Then he took hold of my hand and held it so tightly that I felt, at that moment, I was an anchor for him. Then it came his turn to pray, and his hand squeezed even tighter.

"Dear God, help me get things together in my head," he said. "Help me not to be so messed up," he said. "And, could you help my mother who's going to have an operation today. I hope she knows I love her, God, even if she doesn't love me. And my grandmother too, God? Please help grandma to deal with all her pain and suffering, God. Please do that...."

During the latter part of his prayer, he squeezed my hand very tightly and I had the feeling that there was great emotion behind the words that he was saying.

"And one more thing, God," Terry said. "Please

pray for Covenant House. I'd be lost without this house," he said.

He sat down and squeezed my hand a little tighter still. He never let go. For the rest of the service, especially when the kids got up and sang their own songs from the top of their lungs, he kept gripping my hand. Even now, three hours after I left him, I can still feel it there, I can still see his face.

(By the way, hearing the kids sing is one of the most beautiful things I've ever heard. They pick the songs themselves — songs like "Our God Is an Awesome God," and "Wind Beneath My Wings." They especially like the words to "Wind Beneath My Wings." I've heard a lot of great professionals sing it — but no one does it better than our homeless kids. No one....)

"Thanks, Sister," was all he said when he left. "Thanks."

"You're welcome, Terry," I said. "See you around, I hope," I said.

I can't get Terry, and all the other kids out of my mind. As I sat there next to him today, I became painfully aware of how permeated all their prayers were with suffering and hardships and rejection and fear of the future.

At the same time that they turned to the Lord asking His help, they thanked God over and over, for Covenant House and for the love and care that they found there. And, they prayed not only for the other kids but for the staff and for the donors who keep

Covenant House alive.

I found myself hoping that the faith, confidence, and trust in God that their prayers expressed so plaintively would expand and grow so as to permeate their lives. I thanked God for my own gift of faith and reflected on the joy and consolation that a life of prayer had been for me — consoling me in sadness, sustaining me in this wonderful Covenant House mission, and every day strengthening me for the future.

I also was aware what an opportunity and a call was ours to be instruments of putting these kids back in touch with God. Most had not been to church for ages and had been "disconnected" from everything, including God.

These kids really are beautiful. They really, really are.

Chapter 12

*"This is a picture of me
when I was dead."*

Easter, 1992

"This is a picture of me when I was dead, Sister," he said.

"Look at this, Sister. This is me two years ago ... when I was dead," he said.

I reached out and took the battered ID card from him (we give cards to all our long-term kids every six months so we can keep track of who's in and who's out). The photo showed a tortured face ... a face filled with hopelessness and despair.

Arnie was right. He really did look dead.

"I think you're getting better looking with age, Arnie," I smiled. "I think you're right," he said.

"I'm never going to lose this photo," he said. "I mean, I look at it every day to remind me how far I've come," he said. "And I love comparing it to *this* photo," he said.

Arnie reached into his pocket, and pulled out another ID card. "Here, Sister, look at this ID card ... you're going to love it," he said.

The picture looked just like the Arnie standing

there in front of me — all smiles. But it wasn't an ID card for Covenant House — it was an ID card for the bank he was working for.

"I'm still at the bank, Sister. It's a really good job. Thanks for helping me get it."

"I'm so proud of you, Arnie," I said as I reached out and gave him a hug. "I'm so thrilled for you," I said as I turned to go. But Arnie wouldn't let me.

"I want you to know something, Sister," he said. "I look at these every day ... so I never forget how far I've come," he said. *"These pictures tell it all, Sister. This is the story of my salvation."* I looked up at him, startled by what he said.

"I really mean that, Sister. This is the story of my salvation." Tears were filling in his eyes. "I've got to go see some of the other guys, Sister," he said. I think he was afraid to let me see him crying. "I understand, Arnie," I said.

(And now he is "resurrected." He has New Life.)

He is 19 years old, and he never had a home, and he used to be dead. I'm convinced Arnie is God's Easter present to me and our kids — a living, breathing symbol of the resurrection happening all over again.

It's not easy explaining Easter and the resurrection to our kids. I mean, it's tough for a homeless kid who has been dying on the street to understand the passionate love of the Father or the mystery of His salvation and redemption.

For most of our kids, the harsh reality of their lives doesn't leave much time or much room for wondering about a God who loved them so much He died for them 2,000 years ago. Our kids are overwhelmed with more basic questions — like "what will happen to me tomorrow," "why doesn't anyone love me," ... "will anyone ever love me?"

I think God understands the questions and doubts our kids have better than anyone — that's why He sent Arnie to us. I really think Arnie is a re-enactment of Jesus' Resurrection ... a living and breathing symbol of new life in sneakers and blue jeans.

And when our homeless kids can see and touch and listen to a resurrection like Arnie ... I really think they can begin to hope and believe that a resurrection might one day happen inside them. It means a lot to our kids if they can see it in person.

I know that Arnie is God's Easter present to me, too. There is nothing — absolutely nothing — more beautiful than seeing a child rise to life in front of your eyes. And it's most beautiful of all when that child actually sees the resurrection happening in himself. "These photos tell the story of my salvation, Sister. I look at them every day."

I hope you realize that Arnie is one of God's Easter presents to you, too. I mean, kids like Arnie don't rise out of the quicksand of the streets alone. They absolutely need someone to lift them out. Those are your hands that saved Arnie. I know that Arnie wouldn't be living and breathing today, if you hadn't been there for him during all his past Good Fridays.

I really wish you could have seen him today. I

thank God for helping us bring kids like Arnie back to Him.

I want to again say thank you, for Arnie. Thank you for helping to bring him to me this morning. I really feel fortunate to have met him.

I hope you and all those you love enjoy a blessed and joyous Easter. You've already made ours....

We never stop thanking God you found us.

Chapter 13

"It's my mother's ashes."

June, 1992

She came to our front door Tuesday morning, ragged and dirty clothes on her back, and a little aluminum paint can in her arms.

From the second she stepped inside, she made it clear to us that she and the paint can were a "package deal." *Whatever she did, wherever she went, the little paint can never left her hands.*

When Kathy sat in the crisis shelter, the can sat in her arms. She took the can with her to the cafeteria that first morning she ate, and to bed with her that first night she slept.

When she stepped into the shower, the can was only a few feet away. When she dressed, the can rested alongside her feet.

"I'm sorry, this is mine," she told our counselors, whenever we asked her about it. "This can belongs to me."

"Do you want to tell me what's in it, Kathy," I asked her? "Um, not today," she'd say, and then quietly walked off.

When Kathy was sad, or angry or hurt — which

happened a lot — she took her paint can to a quiet
dorm room on the third floor. Many times on Tuesday
and Wednesday and Thursday, I'd pass by her room,
and watch her rock gently back and forth, the can in
her arms. Sometimes she'd talk to the paint can in low
whispers.

I've been around troubled kids all my life — we'll
see 35,000 homeless kids this year alone. I'm used to
seeing them carry stuffed animals (some of the rough-
est, toughest kids at Covenant House have a stuffed
animal). Every kid has something — needs something
— to hold.

But a paint can? I could feel alarm bells ringing in
my head. I had to reach this kid, and I thought I should
do it now.

Early this morning, I decided to "accidentally" run
into her again. "Would you like to join me for break-
fast," I asked. "That would be great," she said.

For a few minutes we sat in a corner of our cafeteria, talking quietly over the din of 150 ravenous homeless kids. Then I took a deep breath, and plunged into
it....

"Kathy, that's a really nice can. What's in it?"

For a long time, Kathy didn't answer. She rocked
back and forth, her black hair swaying across her
shoulders. Then she looked over at me, tears in her
eyes.

"It's my mother," she said.

"Oh," I said. "What do you mean, it's your
mother?"

"It's my mother's ashes," she said.

"I went and got them from the funeral home. See, I even asked them to put a label right here on the side. It has her name on it."

Kathy held the can up before my eyes. A little label on the side chronicled all that remained of her mother: date of birth, date of death, name. That was it. Then Kathy pulled the can close, and hugged it.

"I never really knew my mother, Sister," Kathy told me. "I mean, she threw me in the garbage two days after I was born." (We checked Kathy's story. Sure enough, the year she was born, the New York newspapers ran a story, saying that police had found a little infant girl in a dumpster ... and yes, it was two days after Kathy was born.)

"I ended up living in a lot of foster homes, mad at my mother," Kathy said. "But then I decided I was going to try to find her. I got lucky — someone knew where she was living. I went to her house."

"She wasn't there, Sister," she said. "My mother was in the hospital. She had AIDS."

"I went to the hospital, and I got to meet her the day before she died. My mother told me she loved me, Sister," Kathy said crying. "That's why I went to get her ashes." (We double-checked Kathy's story ... every word of it was true.)

I reached out and hugged Kathy, and she cried in my arms for a long, long time. It was tough getting my arms around her, because she just wouldn't put the paint can down. But she didn't seem to mind. I know

I didn't.....

I saw Kathy again, a couple hours ago, eating dinner in our cafeteria. She made a point to come up and say hi. I made a point to give her an extra hug....

Chapter 14

"I'm afraid that answer isn't good enough."

July, 1992

"Please sit here, President Bush," I said when he walked into my office.

"Thanks for dropping by to visit, Mr. Clinton," I said.

"This chair would be perfect for you, Mr. Perot," I said.

The three Presidential candidates took their seats in my office, and smiled in unison. It was really something to have all of them at Covenant House together. "What is it you want to talk to us about, Sister?" they asked.

I looked at each of them, and smiled back. I thought I'd be nervous, but I wasn't.

"I want you to know I'm a little disappointed," I told them. "And really bothered." I spread my words around the office, talking to no one in particular but to all of them individually. I could tell they were pretty surprised.

"I mean, I don't want to sound disrespectful. I know each of you really cares a lot about America's

kids. But I feel like our kids are drowning. And unless
something is done now — right away — a whole generation is going to die before our eyes."

"I'm very glad you mentioned that, Sister Mary
Rose," they all said. "I couldn't agree with you more,"
they all said. "I'm giving a speech today which outlines my solution," they said.

"I don't think you really heard me," I said. "I
mean, I've heard thousands of speeches from politicians over the last forty years. I guess I'm just tired of
all the rhetoric — I want action," I said.

"I mean, I feel like our cities and towns have
become like a rushing stream, filled with drowning
kids. I keep reaching down to save them — our donors
keep saving them — but the stream just seems to get
more crowded. I can hear their cries in my sleep.

"And I can't stop asking myself — *"Isn't it time
we did something?* Isn't it time we all walked
upstream to see who and what is throwing these kids
into the water?

As soon as the last words tumbled out of my
mouth, each man looked down at the floor. "I've been
trying to get that done," they all said. "But it's not my
fault," they all said.

"I'm afraid that answer isn't good enough," I said.
"This isn't a political issue — it's a life and death
tragedy affecting thousands of rejected, hurting kids
living on the streets," I said. "These innocent lives
belong to all of us ... we're all responsible."

At that point a bunch of our homeless kids came

in. I was glad that Mr. Bush, Mr. Clinton, and Mr. Perot would get to see the kids up close ... to hear what it felt like to be without a mother, a father, a skill, a job ... a chance.

Then, the alarm went off.

It was 6:00 A.M., and my little dream was over.

* * * * * * * * * * * * * * *

I've got a tiny confession to make. Everything in my letter so far was a dream.

It was nice to dream about doing something really outspoken and different to help our kids ... but it was only a dream. *And ever since I had it, I've been getting angrier and angrier.*

I mean, *I'm tired of dreaming* that the solution is right around the corner.

I'm tired of dreaming that maybe "next year" someone will somehow do something to save America's kids.

I'm tired of holding kids while they cry in my arms ... and feeling like nothing is getting done.

I know you feel the same way too.

So, I've decided to do something about it.

If I can't get Mr. Bush, Mr. Clinton and Mr. Perot into my office at once, I can try to do the next best thing — get their attention! I'm going to make sure they'll hear me ... they'll hear our kids ... they'll hear you!

ANNOUNCING...

An Historic
National Youth Convention
for America's Kids!

Featuring,
National Political Leaders
and real-life testimonies from
America's homeless kids.

July 12, 12:30 P.M.
Covenant House
Ninth Avenue and 17th Street
New York, New York

I'm really excited about this idea. I mean, I can't think of any way you and I can possibly draw more attention to this problem, than to hold this convention the day before the Democrats hold their convention in New York.

(Please, please understand one thing right away. I'm not doing this to pick on the Democrats, or the Republicans, or the Independents, or any political party. As I said before, this issue transcends politics.)

(I *am* doing it because there is a major political convention in New York and the city is going to be filled with thousands of delegates and reporters ... and this is a once-every-four-year opportunity for us to shine the spotlight on America's kids!)

I'm going to state as forcefully as I can that our kids must be a national priority. And, our kids are going to get up and tell all the delegates, politicians and the national media what it feels like to be a homeless kid. And they're going to tell America what it feels like to struggle without a job skill ... to be poor ... and to face drug dealers on every street corner.

They're going to tell the people in power how desperately they need housing, job training, education, and general family support.

I'm not trying to kid anyone. I realize that this one event will not solve the problem by itself. But, it's a start.

I'm convinced it will make a difference. It will draw attention ... it will focus responsibility ... on a national tragedy which threatens an entire generation of American kids.

And, I'd also like to give *you* a chance to make a real difference. (If you share my frustration about what's happening to our country's kids, this is your chance!!!)

First, join us on July 12th. Our auditorium seats 900 people and we'd really like you to be here with us. Seating is limited though, so pick up the phone today, and call Joseph at 1-800-388-3888, to reserve your seat.

Second ... even if you can't come, I'm praying you'll still stand up and tell America's candidates to take notice ... by signing the slip I've enclosed. Just sign it and get it back to me. Make it clear to

America's politicians that you intend to vote this year
... for someone who is committed to making the rescue
of our kids a national priority.

I'm hoping to collect 100,000 signatures in July so
I can take our case — our concerns — our frustrations
— to Washington, D.C. Please join us.

And *Third*, please join me in saying a prayer for
this event ... and send a donation if you can, to help
our kids.

*In a world where talk is cheap, you've been like a
genuine national treasure to our kids.* Your very beautiful donations have been tangible, real, life-saving
gifts to our desperate kids. Every time you have given
to Covenant House, you have stood up, and helped
save a human life. God bless you for that! So please,
send a donation to help during this busy summer, if
you can.

I know this is a very unusual request — but I think
we live in a time and place where it's up to you and me
to do whatever it takes to help our kids.

I'm tired of dreaming. I want action.

Please ... join our Youth Convention to save our
kids today. Please. Our kids will be praying for you
tonight. They — we — never, ever stop thanking God
you found us!

*P.S. Every time I think this problem is too overwhelm-
ing ... that it's too big for one person like me to
make a difference, I look at this clipping I keep on
my desk: "On the street I saw a small girl cold and*

shivering in a thin dress, with little hope of a decent meal. I became angry and said to God: "Why did you permit this? Why don't you do something about it?" For a while God said nothing. That night He replied quite suddenly: 'I certainly did something about it. I made you.'"

Chapter 15

"I got no other choice, Sister.
I do it to survive."

September, 1992

During the day, his name is Tommy. But when darkness falls, he puts on a red halter top, a black leather skirt and transforms himself....

The little boy becomes a five-foot-five-inch "sex kitten" dressed in girls' clothes.

The little boy is 12 years old.

"Hi. Can I have a cup of lemonade, please?" he asked last night. "Could I please?" It was 2:30 in the morning, and we were sitting inside the Covenant House van. His manners were impeccable.

"Of course," I said. "I don't think we've met," I said. My name is Sister Mary Rose."

"My name is Delilah," the little boy said. "Thanks for the lemonade, Sister. Thanks," he said.

He took the cup in his tiny hands, and gulped it down. For a moment, his eyes zeroed in on me, but quickly turned away. Even after just ten seconds, I could tell he was very shy, and very, very uncomfortable.

"I hope you don't mind if I stay in here a few extra

minutes tonight, Sister," he said. "I'm really tired."

"Of course not," I said. "I'd really like to talk to you."

He looked up at me again, then turned and peered out the window. "There's not much to tell you," he said.

He turned and smiled. I began to talk, but he got his words out first....

"I hope you understand, Sister. I don't like doing this. I really, really don't. I got no other choice, Sister. I do it to survive."

He looked up at me, pleading for me to understand.

"I mean, it's not like I got a lot of choices, you know. My Mom and Dad are both dead, Sister. Ever since last summer, I've been on my own. I don't know anyone...."

"Then I met some guy, and he told me if I dressed up like this I could make a lot of money. So, I ... I did it."

"You can come back with us, Delilah. We'll help you," I said. "We'd really like to help you."

"I'd ... I might want to do that someday," he said. "I just don't know if I should ... I'm all right on my own, Sister" he said. "I think I'll be okay...."

God, I hope we can reach this kid soon. Time is running out.

"I'm not going to do any drinking ... I'm not going to do drugs ... I'm going to stay clean," Tommy had told our van team six months ago. Back then, we'd spot him outside just one night a week, maybe twice. We've really been keeping an eye on him.

But now, he's out on the streets every night. I can see the streets eating him up before my eyes. A couple of weeks back, we heard that Tommy was experimenting with drugs. "He's doing it to forget what he's doing," one of the kids told me.

I wish I was able to make better sense of all this. I mean, when I look at a kid like Tommy, I don't see a pre-teen prostitute ... I see a 12-year-old boy who's all alone, just trying to survive. Somehow. Some way. I see a desperate child of God so embittered with his world, that he'll do things you and I can't imagine, just to stay alive.

One thing I know for sure, though, is that God wants me to *believe* in Tommy. There is absolutely no one else who will ... who can help him right now, except us. No one....

Please ... do you think you could say an extra prayer for Tommy tonight? And while you're at it, do you think you could remember the kids who are sleeping safe and sound in our shelter tonight, the kids who have started to make it back. They all need your prayers, especially Tommy....

"Good bye, Sister," he said to me as he got out of our van tonight. "I'll be seeing you around, okay?"

"Good bye," I said as he walked out into the darkness. "Take care of yourself," I said. I could feel a huge lump in my throat.

We never give up on kids like Tommy. Every

night we look for him and hope that tonight's the night ... that he'll be ready to come back with us: that we'll finally be able to help him.

Please, let us pray that he finds his way to our shelter.

Chapter 16

*"The boy was even scared
to look at himself because he thought
that his own reflection
would make fun of him."*

October, 1992

I've had a really tough time writing you this month. Every time I start typing, my eyes fill up and I have to stop.

I mean, I usually get pretty emotional writing you these stories, but this month's has really hit me hard. Please, let me tell you what's happened (and promise me you'll read this all the way through, no matter how tough it gets. Please. It's really important....)

It all started about eight o'clock this morning, when I was sitting in my office, trying to catch up on the hundred or so things that needed to be caught up on, when my secretary, Pat, walked in. She looked really shaken.

"I don't know if you've seen this yet, Sister," she said, handing me a stack of bright pink pages. "It's the latest issue of 'Message,'" she said. ("Message" is the newsletter our kids put out about themselves — a place they share stories, poems, reflections. It can get pretty deep sometimes.) "I must have read this part about ten times last night," Pat said.

There, on page 5, was a short story written by one of our kids named Frankie. Even now, after reading it countless times myself, I still have trouble believing it....

Nightmares of Life
by Frankie

This is a story about nightmares that I have had. I remember one nightmare I had, when I was just a kid.

It was a dark night, my stepfather was babysitting my baby brother and my mother was working in a pizza shop. My brother was sleeping and I was watching television. My father called me to the kitchen where he was watching a pornographic movie. He told me that he wanted me to be like the woman in the movie, but I said no.

He said that if I didn't do what he told me to do he would use my brother. So I told him not to do that to my baby brother, that I would do it. So my stepfather used me as though I was a woman and he forced me to do things I didn't want to do. I had to or else he would have done it to my brother.

The next day I woke up scared and thought it was a nightmare but it wasn't cause I found blood on my underwear and I was naked. I still remember that night but I'm a survivor. I will never let anything get in my way 'cause of what happened in my past. For three years I had nightmares of torture, but I am still a survivor.

I put the kids' newsletter down for a moment, then picked it up and read it, then put it down again. Then, I looked away from the copy and turned to God, Frankie's true, loving father and begged him to let Frankie trust us, and let us help him. The hurt is so deep, it indeed will take God's healing to help him get past it.

On page 18 was another story by Frankie, a story entitled "The Lonely Child."

The Lonely Child

The Lonely Child is a story about a boy who was abused by all his family members. The boy once wished that he was in another world, but it was all just a dream.

He imagined that he played with aliens that would come and pick up little abused kids and take them to another planet where nobody would bother the kids. But it was only a dream.

He tried to feel happy, but he couldn't because he just thought about what his stepfather did to him or what his mother, real father or what his friends did to him. The boy was even scared to look at himself because he thought that his own reflection would make fun of him. He remembers the day he entered the bathroom and saw his stepfather. He realized that he was the boy who was raped and beaten by his stepfather. The boy couldn't do anything except what his stepfather told him to do. The boy couldn't sleep for days, trying to forget what had happened to him, only tears came down his face. As time passed, the boy was thinking he could end this but he couldn't.

The boy still thinks about what happened in his childhood. He still cries on the inside, and outside he knows that he's still a lonely child. The boy still needs someone to tell him that they love him and that they will not hurt his feelings.

The boy's name is Frankie. Now I love myself and I can look at myself in the mirror and say to myself that I will always look beautiful and that someone in this world will love me.

I can't stop thinking about Frankie's letters. It really tears me up inside....

I mean, there's something very final, very cold and undeniable, about reading words like this.

Every week I listen to stories of abuse and pain and neglect, told to me by lots of kids. But at least with these kids I can reach out and be there in that excruciating moment of pain. I can hold them and smile and pray with them that somehow, some way, things will get better for them. I get to experience the incredible joy of seeing some of these kids smile back.

But Frankie's two letters? I can't imagine what it must have been like for him to sit in a room, all alone, and write about his nightmares, much less experience them.

How did it feel for this poor kid to write about a nightmare that you know deep down will still be alongside you in bed tonight, and every other night for the rest of your life?

How did it feel to ache so much, that you spend your childhood dreaming about "aliens that would come and pick up little abused kids and take them to another planet where nobody would bother the kids?"

How does it feel to have to acknowledge to yourself that you're scared to look in a mirror because you're afraid "my own reflection will make fun of me?"

I think these two short stories written by a teenage, homeless kid in a 30-page pink newsletter sum up the pain all our kids feel.

Some of them, like Frankie, have blessedly reached a point where they can at least talk about their nightmares, and write about them, and hopefully one day put them aside (although you and I know the pain will never really leave, it will just hide somewhere.)

For most of our other kids, the ones who are even

more lost, more hurt, more unwilling or unable to deal
with their own nightmares, they're the ones who hurt
even more. I worry about them most of all....

Chapter 17

*"I guess some people might think
you and I are a little crazy."*

Christmas, 1992

On the day before we celebrate His birth under the star of Bethlehem, Jesus will walk, unannounced, into Covenant House.

I know this will happen because it happened last year, and the year before.

He'll show up at our door around six o'clock in the evening....

"Hi," a scared kid in sneakers will say. "Um, my name is Brian, and I was just wondering if, uh, if you had any room tonight. Could I come in Sister? Could I? Please?"

"Hi Brian ... and welcome," I'll say. "Of course we have room for you." ("Hi! Welcome Jesus," is what I'll be thinking.)

I guess some people might think you and I are a little crazy, because we see Jesus on the tired face of a street kid, standing in torn sneakers, wrapped in dirty clothes.

But it's not hard to see Him in all our kids. I remember the baby of Bethlehem, born into similar straits: cold, hungry, homeless. I remember that even as a man, He was an outcast, shunned by the rich and powerful.

And I remember those words He left us, "Whatever you do to the least of my brethren, you do to me" (Matthew 25:40). I think those words come alive for me on Christmas Eve more than any other. Every time I see a kid, I remember that Jesus said He would always be with us, and He'd always be inside each one of us ... even kids like Brian. Maybe, *especially* kids like Brian?

By 7:00 P.M. on Christmas Eve, we'll be dragging out the sleeping bags, and trying to figure out where to put all the kids. By 8:00 P.M., Covenant House will be a madhouse. If you think your local shopping mall is crowded on Christmas Eve, you should see this place at about 8:00 P.M. on the 24th.

It's hectic, it's wonderful ... and it's very, very sad.

I think I love Christmas as much as anyone in the world, but it's pretty hard to handle at Covenant House — for us, and the kids. We'll do all we can for the kids ... we'll sing Christmas carols, and eat good food, and talk about peace and joy.

And the kids will do their best to pretend — for one night — that everything is all right (I think the kids pretend just to make us feel good.) They'll hug counselors and other kids. They'll wish each other "Merry Christmas!" They'll do their best — as well as a homeless-never-loved-before-on-Christmas-day kid can — to ignore the all-consuming pain in their lives.

And I swear they'll wake up early, just like kids do on Christmas morning all over the world, hoping there's something good under the tree. (Thanks to you, there will be.)

The rest of Christmas day? Our Christmas prayer service will be packed. And when we ask the kids if they'd like to pray for someone, I'm going to get a huge lump in my throat....

"Please, Dear God," a kid will say, "help my parents to get along better." "Please, Dear God," another will say, "help my sister, who really needs the help." "Please, Dear God," one more will say, "Please let me spend next Christmas with a family that loves me. Is that asking too much God?"

After prayers, the kids won't talk much about their emptiness — Christmas is too precious a moment of pure joy for kids who've known too little joy in their lives. And I won't let on how much I hurt for them, even though I'll cry a lot inside.

For one day, I want them all to experience the joy of being a kid. A kid who doesn't have the weight of the world on their shoulders. A kid who feels at peace. If only for one day....

Of course, you make it all possible for our kids that day. So, thanks to you, when Jesus comes to our door on Christmas Eve, we'll welcome Him with a big hug. We'll feed Him, give Him a place to sleep, and make sure He feels loved. For one day, we'll make sure all the homeless, lonely Jesuses have a home ... and a small bit of "Peace on Earth." Thanks to you....

God bless you! And may you and those you love enjoy a most blessed Christmas. Our kids and I will be praying for you.

P.S. I hope you can join us at our Midnight Mass at 11:30 on Christmas Eve. We start singing carols in the chapel at 11:00 P.M. Please call Joseph at 800-388-3888, if you can make it, so we'll expect you.

Perhaps the greatest gift a kid can get on Christmas day is to know someone really loves them, and cares about them, tattered clothes and all. Do you think maybe you could let our kids know that you're thinking of them this Christmas? I've enclosed a card, and left room where you can write your own Christmas greeting. Please just get it back to me before Christmas, and I'll make sure a kid gets it this Christmas Eve. Thanks again so much.

Chapter 18

*"God, I can't believe
they did this to me."*

January, 1993

The cab hurtled down 10th Avenue, careened onto a sidewalk on 41st, and then screeched to a dead stop in front of our shelter.

"I got a kid here," the cab driver blurted out, leaping onto the sidewalk. "I got a kid here ... geez, she's in really bad shape ... she gave me 20 bucks to bring her here. Geeeeez, look at her ... she's just a kid."

Even though the cabby was yelling at the top of his lungs, we could barely hear him. The screaming in the back seat was so loud.

From the sidewalk, in the eerie 2:00 A.M. blackness, we couldn't see the girl in the back seat. Simultaneously enraged, devastated, and terrified, she had curled herself into a tightly-wound ball and hidden herself on the floor of the cab.

"I can't believe they did this to me," she kept screeching at the top of her voice. "God, I can't believe they did this to me."

When our counselors were finally able to coax her out of the back seat, we carried her safely inside.

Fresh bruises covered every inch of her legs.

The kid looked barely 15 years old.

For the next three hours, she did all she could, as loudly as she could, to tell the world how much she hurt inside. Once, for five minutes, she stopped screaming and crying long enough to take a deep breath, but it was only a temporary reprieve for her and for us. It wasn't until daylight broke over the shelter that she fell into sleep.

For the next 12 hours she slept, tossing and turning. Finally, early the next afternoon, the girl pried her eyes open, looked around, and began to cry.

"I can't believe they did this to me," she kept sobbing into her pillow. "I can't believe anyone could be that cruel...."

I reached out and grabbed her hand, told her it was all right to cry. "You're safe now," I told her. "We want to help you," I said. "We're so sorry," I said.

She looked up at me, dripping in tears, biting her top lip as hard as she could to keep it all inside. "I'm so scared," she said. "I'm so scared."

"We'll take care of you," I said. "Can you tell us what happened?"

"I'm ... I'm too ashamed to tell you," the little girl said. "I ... I don't think you'll like me if I tell you."

"Try me," I smiled. I was beginning to feel a little scared.

"I'm ... I'm a prostitute," she said. The tears were gushing out faster than ever.

"I mean ... I don't want to do that ... I hate it ... I

hate it. But I don't have any choice," she said. "My boyfriend says he'll kill me if I don't stay on the street....

"He said he'd kill me," she said.

"What happened last night?" I asked as gently as I could.

"I was on the street ... I had to make extra money tonight ... he was screaming at me as loud as he could ... even though I'd been beat up the night before....

"A cab pulled up ... a man asked me to get in ... he said he'd give me $20 if I did something with him in the cab. I ... needed the money ... I...." For the next five minutes the little girl lay in the bed writhing in tears, sobbing uncontrollably, choking out of breath, watching the horror replay in her head again and again. All I could do was pat her on her back and say how sorry I was. It hardly seemed enough....

"You don't have to go on," I told her. "I understand, I said. "I understand."

"I want to tell you the rest ... I need to tell you what happened," she said.

"I ... did things with the man, while the cab driver drove around. I took the $20 and just jumped out of the cab. I couldn't wait to get away from there.

"As I got out of the car I knew I couldn't do it anymore. I was sick and angry ... and I hurt all over. So, I jumped in another cab, gave the driver the $20 and said take me to Covenant House. I just couldn't take it any more....

"I can't take it anymore. I can't believe my

boyfriend made me do this. He said he cared about me," she screamed.

For the past 48 hours we've hovered over the little girl, keeping watch, protecting her from the hate she feels for herself. In dribs and drabs, between the round-the-clock tears, we've been able to piece together her story.

Her name is Melissa. She's 16 years old. She's from Nebraska. Three years ago, after a terrible fight with her mother, she packed $327 and some clothes into a backpack and ran away with a much-older "boyfriend."

For the past three years, she's been under the watchful eye of "Sweetpea," a very grimy excuse for a human being who plies the sexual trade on the Minnesota Strip. Mr. Sweetpea is about to hear from us....

As for Melissa and her parents? Melissa promises us she's going to call tomorrow (we're giving her a few days to work up the courage). Until then, all of us are saying extra prayers hoping for the best. Dear God, she is only a 16-year-old girl. She desperately needs her family right now....

I want to thank you for doing what you did to help us rescue this poor child. I mean, your prayers and donations keep us here every night, letting kids know that a safe haven called Covenant House is only a desperate cab ride away. Your prayers and donations put the food in Melissa's stomach, the clean clothes on her back, the round-the-clock counseling at her fingertips.

You helped save her, you really did. I mean if it hadn't been for you and Covenant House where else would Melissa have escaped?

Thank you. And God bless you. And please, if you can, say a prayer as we begin this new year. This year, thousands of kids will come to us — on foot, via subway, or scrunched in the back seat of a beat-up old cab. Please pray that these kids will find us before it's too late. Your prayers really do bring them to us, you know. They really do.

And thanks for one more thing — letting Melissa find us. We never stop thanking God you found us every day.

Chapter 19

*"She said those other kids
were worth more than me."*

February, 1993

He walked right up to me, and launched into it without any preambles. He was 16 years old, and he was a little desperate and very tired, so he decided to get right to the point.

"Sister, how much do you get paid to take care of me," he asked.

"I mean, how much does the state give you. Do they give you a lot?"

I could tell by Ricky's face there was something in this question much deeper than a curiosity about the finances of Covenant House. It isn't often a 16 year old gets curious about who pays for the food and rent.

"Why do you want to know, Ricky?"

"Well, it's just ... I was just wondering."

"Are you worried about something?"

"Well, I figured that if you were getting paid by the state to take care of me, then you'd probably keep me around.

"I mean, you'd have to keep me around to get the money, right?" He bit off the word "have" for extra emphasis.

How on earth do these kids become so jaded so fast?

When Ricky walked in here yesterday, we didn't ask him a lot of questions about his past. We wanted to make sure he felt welcome. He told us he was 16 and that he had been on the streets for six months ... ever since his mother threw him out of the house.

He was so exhausted when he walked in that he could barely keep his eyes open. He said he had a hard time sleeping on the streets because he was scared all the time. He said there were very scary people on the streets.

He just woke up from his safe bed at Covenant House a little while ago, after sleeping for almost 24 hours.

"Ricky, money has nothing to do with it. I would want you here if I didn't have a penny in the world. We love you. Now, why did you ask that question?"

"Well ... that's what my mother said when she threw me out. She said she got money from the state for the foster children she took in and if I was gone she could take in one more foster child.

"So she told me to get out. She said she wasn't making any money on me. I'm her son! She said those other kids were worth more than me. She told *me* to get out, Sister!"

Ricky looked up at me, lost in his words. Tears rolled down his face. "Can you believe that Sister," he kept saying. "Can you believe that?"

I reached out for him, and hugged him for a minute. I could believe it.... Tragically, I hear stories like this all too often. But it doesn't make Ricky's story any easier to accept....

Answers? Solutions? I don't have any.

I wish I did, but I don't. Because of the spiraling breakdown of the American family, more and more kids are freefalling alone, without the safety net of a place to call home. Because of massive budget cuts, programs to help these kids are becoming increasingly invisible. (When budgets get cut, children's programs are traditionally cut to bits. Kids don't march, they don't vote, they don't send money to political campaigns.)

And while the need grows and the "means" shrink, an incredibly dedicated, well-meaning but shrinking army of overworked, underappreciated social workers are doing their best to find a place for these kids.

Somehow, amidst all the good intentions, kids become little living and breathing commodities. Some slip through the cracks. Some, like Ricky, are literally pushed out their front door, and told to make it on their own. It's terrible, it's wrong, and it hurts.

And once again, Covenant House stands as the last stop at the end of the dead-end street, ready to pick up the pieces.

I really didn't know how to answer Ricky's question. So I gave him the only answer I could.

"Ricky, we'll always be here for you, no matter what. There is no one more valuable than you in the entire world. You are priceless. I know that, and I'll never forget it. You don't have to worry now."

I think I caught him a little by surprise. "Thanks, Sister," he said. "You mean it?" he said. "That's really nice," he said.

"Our pleasure," I said. I saw Ricky again about an hour ago, and he ducked around a corner. I think he's still afraid we might change our mind and tell him it's time to leave.

I'll make sure I give him more reassurance tomorrow. Until then, thanks for praying for him, if you can. We never, ever stop thanking God you found us.

P.S. I tried to avoid Ricky's questions about funding because I thought if I told him that Covenant House was funded by people like you who send money out of love, he'd be worried. He doesn't trust love anymore. He wants to know that someone is obligated to care for him. I know you aren't personally obligated, but in a way we're all obligated as God's children. That's why we'll never turn a child away no matter how tight money is. I count on you for help. Will you please send a gift this month. Thanks!

Chapter 20

"Tiene usted una madre, Hermana?"
(Do you have a mother?)
she asked shyly.

April, 1993
Nebaj, Guatemala

It's siesta time here in Nebaj, Guatemala, but all the kids are out playing.

Right now, I'm in a little room, which consists of a table with one broken leg, three folding chairs, a coffee maker (our one indulgence), a rickety desk and an old Remington.

And I'm sitting in one of those rusty chairs, pecking away at this creaky typewriter, trying to put my feelings into words.

Being here, in this wounded, war-torn nation, has been such a frightening and deeply-moving experience that I'm almost at a loss to describe it.

But somehow, I felt I had to try to communicate it to you.

Because now I know, to the very core of my being, that this is work God wants us to do.

That the children who live in this wretched and forsaken land are His children, as much His "Holy

Innocents" as the kids who roam the streets of New York, New Orleans or Los Angeles.

I know I haven't told you much about our efforts in Central America. I guess I don't talk about it much because it feels so far away. And, in some ways, it is. This place is a world apart from the streets of Manhattan.

For one thing, the kids we care for are almost all under the age of 12. Some are as young as seven years old — the age for playing soccer, or learning their ABCs.

The thing these kids in Nebaj have in common is that they are all orphans. Their parents have been killed, innocent victims of bloody political battles and civil wars.

Worse yet, many of these children were forced to stand and watch their parents being killed.

If the child cried out, or closed his eyes, the brutality worsened. In the end, the parents' suffering was so unbearable, their children prayed for them to die.

What these innocent children have endured is truly beyond imagining.

I know this must be upsetting for you. But I am leading to something ... so please bear with me.

You see, despite all that has happened to these children, when I look into their eyes, I see hope. These children aren't closed and bitter — they long to love and be loved.

It's one of the most incredible things I've ever witnessed.

I hadn't been here in Nebaj for 10 minutes before I got my first glimpse of their compassion and kindness.

It was late in the afternoon, and I had just arrived after a grueling plane ride over the mountains. I was sitting on the steps to the house — a simple, wooden compound with beds for 14 children and six workers — trying to catch my breath.

An Indian child about 11 years old, with huge, saucer eyes approached me cautiously. I smiled and she sat down by my side.

"Tiene usted una madre, Hermana?" (Do you have a mother?) she asked shyly.

"Yes, I do," I replied. "But she's in heaven."

She nodded in grave understanding. "Do you have a father?"

"Well, yes ... but he's in heaven too."

She put her little hand in mine.

"Then you and I are the same," she said tenderly. "I am Maria ... I don't have any parents, either." And she stood up and put her arms around my neck and hugged me with all her might.

It was all I could do to stop myself from bursting into tears. And I don't consider myself a person who cries easily.

Within seconds, Maria ran to get the other children, shouting, "The sister is just like us."

Before I knew it, I had eight children patting me on the back, touching my hair, and comforting me, as if I had just entered a secret club.

In fact, I had entered a club. You see, I had the

secret password. Orphan. I found out later that's the first question these kids ask every stranger.

"Tiene usted una madre y padre?"

That phrase is going to haunt me for a long, long time.

Now, no one can replace the parents these children have lost. Neither can we wipe away the trauma these children have experienced.

But what we can do is prove that, in a world that can be unspeakably cruel, love still exists. And even though their parents have been taken from them, they can find a new family ... with us.

Can you see why I'm so certain God wants us to be here?

Without Covenant House, I shudder to think what would have happened to Maria. Or Tomas, Consuelo, Juan, Ana or Pablo ... all the "Holy Innocents" that have found refuge in Covenant House in Nebaj.

Now, I have to come to the part I hate the most — the part where I have to reach out my hand to you, palm open, and ask for your help.

These children are fighting for their lives. Their only weapons are hope, and faith ... and you.

"Vaya con Dios," is an expression that's used all the time down here. It means "Go with God." God is watching these children, I know it. That's why He sent us you, and gave you such a compassionate heart.

God bless you, and thank you for caring about our kids.

P.S. I wish I knew the words to describe how beautiful these children are. I just know that, if I could only express it properly, you would want to reach out and take these innocent little ones into your arms, and your heart. They need you so much. I really hope you're able to help.

Chapter 21

*"My new life begins in
just twenty-six days, Sister...."*

May, 1993

"I knew I was in trouble Sister, the second my Father stopped the car."

He kept screaming at the top of his lungs, 'I'm going to kill you kid, I'm going to kill you.' Then he reached down, and grabbed a little container of gasoline ... and he poured it all over me.

"Then he jumped out of the car, lit a match and threw it.

"That's why I look like this now...."

The lanky boy unfolded his six-foot-two-inch frame from a chair in the corner of my office, and lifted up his T-shirt. Old scar tissue from a horrible burn stretched and twisted across his stomach. My eyes started to fill up just looking at it.

"I tried to get out of the car, Sister, but the doors were locked. My Father had locked them. I was finally able to break a window with my elbow, and roll outside on the road. My Father wouldn't take me to the hospital. My skin hurt me for months."

"I'm sorry, Cliff," I finally said, barely containing

my anger. Cliff shrugged as if to say there was nothing anyone could do about it now. It was history. Sad history.

"What about your Mom? Where was she in all this?"

I guess I was looking for some explanation of Cliff's sunny personality. He was such a nice kid. So positive. So upbeat. I liked him immediately.

"Well, Sister, you see, I was adopted, you know. Both of my new parents are really crazy. Did the doctors tell you that yet?" I nodded my head. Our staff has been working overtime talking about Cliff and how we can help him.

"They had a ton of problems. Really, really bad problems." Cliff bit off the last "really" extra hard for emphasis.

"Well, anyway, my Mom never hurt me. She never did. Well, she never hurt me physically, anyway, if you know what I mean."

"How did she hurt you, Cliff," I asked. Alarm bells were ringing extra loud in my head.

"Well, my Mom ... my Mom used to pace up and down the same floor in our house. She'd do it for hours and hours every day. So I used to ... I ...

Cliff paused and bit his lip. "Never mind, Sister. This will sound really stupid."

A huge, single tear began to form in Cliff's left eye. And then this very big, very good kid began to weep.

I reached out and hugged him. "It's okay, Cliff," I

said. "You don't have to tell me," I said. "I under-stand."

"No, you can't understand," he said. "You see, I used to ... when I was a kid I used to lay down on my stomach and stretch out my hands on the floor. Then, when my Mother would walk by, she'd walk right over my hands sometimes."

"I know ... I know how stupid that must sound. But that's the only time I can ever remember my Mom touching me."

I've been caring for kids my whole adult life. More than 45 years (and God willing, many, many more.) But this was one of the saddest stories I ever heard. I reached out and hugged him as hard as I could.

For three long hours Cliff sat in my office that afternoon, telling me his life story. He told me about the times he tried to kill himself. And about the time he packed his bags at 17 and ran away to Chicago.

And he told me about coming to New York, and getting mugged at the Port Authority, and having his eardrum injured.

And he told me how one cold evening, all alone, eardrum hurting, not a penny in his pocket, he sat down on the sidewalks of New York, and cried his eyes out. It was the first time he remembered crying in years.

"That day was the turning point, Sister," he told me one day. "That's the day I found Covenant House ... that's the day it all changed."

And when he left my office, he turned around and faced me with a quiet dignity only a few people on this earth will ever have, and he stood erect and saluted me. "My new life begins in just twenty-six days, Sister," he smiled. "I just got to hang in there twenty-six days."

You see, there are a few other things you should know about Cliff right away ... a few more extraordinary things about a very extraordinary kid.

First of all, Cliff is an out-and-out genius. I mean, a real, certifiable, only-a-handful-of-people-like-him genius.

The second thing you should know, is that in twenty-six days Cliff will ship off to Hawaii and begin a bright new career in the Navy. (By the way, Cliff flunked his hearing test twice before his ear improved enough for him to get accepted. It may have something to do with the fact he spent literally 65 hours "practicing" for his hearing test in our clinic....)

I can't even begin to tell you how proud I am of this kid. And how thankful I am for you, too. I mean, when you get right down to it, Cliff simply wouldn't be beginning a new life in twenty-six days, if Covenant House wasn't here for him. And we couldn't have been here for Cliff, if you weren't there for us. You do know that, I hope! Don't you?

So, please, smile a little extra when you put down this letter tonight. Maybe give yourself an extra pat on the back. The simple, wonderful, undeniable fact is that amidst all the uncertainty and turmoil in this world, you reached out and gave a kid — a total stranger — a chance. A hope. A love he never knew before. A new life, he never dreamed would exist.

Thank you, thank you, thank you so much for this extraordinary gift you have given. We never, ever stop thanking God you found us. I know Cliff will never forget you....

Epilogue

In the time it takes you to read this sentence, a child in America will drop out of school.

In the time it takes you to finish this sentence, another child will run away from home.

In the time it takes you to read this little page, another teenage girl will have a baby.

What does it all mean? Well, I'm sure you understand that the real horror in these facts is not the statistics themselves. It's the knowledge that behind every one of these "numbers" is a flesh and blood kid. A kid who cries like you and I do, who hurts like you and I do, who is utterly scared and terrified every bit as much as you and I would be if we had to walk for a night in their shoes.

And our streets are filled with these flesh and blood victims. As you read this, there are literally hundreds of thousands of kids "out there" on America's streets. Lost and alone. Completely on their own. Hungry. Sick. Scared.

There are two things you should know about these kids.

First, they come from everywhere. From the north and south, the cities and suburbs, from the ghettoes and the poshest neighborhoods. There is no such thing as a "typical" homeless kid. They are as young as eight, and as "old" as 21. They are white, black, Hispanic and Asian. They come from every religious group and they come to us in all shapes and sizes.

But as different as they are, they all have one thing in common: none of these kids wants to be homeless.

Asking for help is never easy, especially asking someone you've never met before. But these kids are so very desperate. And your help now, today, could mean so very much in their lives.

Please ... if it's possible, please help them today, if you can. Please. Thank you, and God bless you.

> In God's love,
> Sister Mary Rose McGeady
> For the kids

A Gift To Be Embraced

Reflections on the
Covenant House Faith Community

The following was written by Alec Aspinwall, a former member of the Covenant House Faith Community in New York City.

Even after making the decision to visit the Covenant House Faith Community in New York City, I have to admit I was still somewhat suspicious. The closer I got to the address on Eighth Avenue in the heart of Times Square, in fact, the more my questions grew. What would draw normal people away from their comfortable lifestyles to pray for three hours a day and work with street kids while making $12 a week? What was drawing me?

For some time I had been searching for a way to deepen my relationship with God, and there was certainly something pushing me to take a closer look. Now, that courage seemed foolish and even a little frightening as I stood on the doorstep waiting for someone to answer the bell. I tried to look nonchalant, but as I glanced across the street, my eyes read the invitation posted on the door of the porno theater and I turned away in disgust — but without success. All around me, as I looked to the left and then to the right, the sorry sights and sounds of a string of "adult entertainment centers" made my stomach turn. I felt stunned. Is this where I had to live if I wanted to feel closer to God? Was I crazy? The eyes of the street people told me what I already knew. "You don't belong here," they said. They were right. I didn't belong there.

Then the door opened, and I was met with a warm smile. I tried to contain my gratitude for the timely rescue.

Once inside I was surprised by the size of the dwelling. It consisted of two six-story buildings joined by a large chapel. The dormitory-style living was neither elegant nor impoverished, but quite plain. The people I was soon to meet, however, were anything but plain.

I found myself in the midst of a Christian "melting pot." There were nurses, teachers, nuns, businesspeople, laborers, retired mothers, and recent college graduates. They had come from all over the country and even from abroad. Although Catholic in prayer and worship, the Community also had members from various Christian denominations. There were conservatives and liberals, rich and not so rich, young and the young at heart. Each had a different story to tell as to why they had come to Covenant House, but their differences were united by the call to strengthen their relationship with one God. To do so, they were willing to accept the challenge of intense prayer (three hours a day), communal living, and working with the kids of

Covenant House, whose lifestyle on the street can make them pretty tough to deal with at times. They hurt so much that sometimes the only way they can feel better about themselves is to hurt you instead.

I had also expected Community members to be a solemn bunch, bearing the weight of the pervasive tragedy that surrounded them — but I found just the opposite to be true. The Community had a vibrant spirit that was full of life and laughter. Somehow the pain they were daily exposed to had actually made room for joy. I'm not saying that I didn't perceive their own suffering, for many of them shared with me the struggles they were experiencing with the kids of Covenant House and with themselves. But they were beginning to see their struggle no longer as a punishment to be endured, but as a gift to be embraced. I began to think that there might be something to that line from the Gospel about how "dying to yourself will bring new life."

By the end of the week, I had a lot to think and pray about. Was I ready to commit to a minimum of 13 months of three hours a day of prayer? Could I dedicate myself to a simple lifestyle in a chaste community? Was I able to let go of the stability offered by my loved ones and my career? Was I willing to be sent to any one of the Covenant House sites assigned to me and work at any job, whether it was working directly with the kids or not? Most of all, could I really love those hardened street kids and let myself be touched by their pain?

I went home to California and asked God to give me a sign. Something simple. An eclipse maybe! No sign came. What did come, finally, was a sense of peace that told me it was all right to go against all the norms and ambitions ingrained in me and take a step forward in faith. After receiving a letter from the Orientation Director, I gave notice at my job and began to make plans to come back to New York.

It's hard to believe I've been here a year now. I've learned so much about myself, the kids, and God. I've learned, for instance, that drawing closer to God is a constant challenge and process. Street kids, I've come to learn, really have soft centers underneath those hard exteriors, and they often have more to teach me than I them. And God is always there, even though sometimes I don't recognize Him.

I still don't like the neighborhood, and I still get the same stares on the street that I did a year ago. Only now, sometimes I see Christ behind the cold eyes, and He reassures me, "You do belong here."

If you would like more information about joining the Faith Community, please write to Orientation Director of Faith Community, 346 West 17th Street, New York, NY 10011-5002, or call (212) 727-4000.

Family
Survival
Guide

*Reflections on
Raising Kids Today*

You've Got a Tough Job.

Most of us were never taught to be parents. So we can't help but disappoint ourselves sometimes. How often have you heard yourself using the very words you hated hearing from your own parents?

And when our kids become teenagers, it gets even harder. They seem to reject everything we've taught them. As far as they're concerned, we know nothing. Our values and beliefs are constantly challenged. Every word we utter is seen as interference. Emotions run high.

But we're more important to our teens than ever. As they try out the values of their peers, who are more influential than ever, we counter the pull of drugs and alcohol. These entangle children every day and can ruin their lives.

The Stakes Are High.

Teenagers who don't get what they need at home look elsewhere. Some run away from home. Many more consider other ways of running from pressure — a once bright and happy son escapes to drugs, a vivacious daughter starts drinking. Think about these facts:

- Each year, one million students drop out of high school or are chronically truant.

- Four out of 10 teenage girls will become pregnant before age 20.

- Although marijuana use has declined in the past years, addiction to cocaine, especially crack, has doubled.

- One in four teens develops a drinking problem during his teen years; about 10,000 will die in alcohol-related accidents this year.

- Each year, 5,000 to 6,000 teens die in suicide-related deaths, and the number is growing, one every 90 minutes. For every death, at least 100 other young people attempt suicide.

The Turbulent Teens.

Teens face many pressures that adults don't take seriously. Their bodies are changing — they have to adjust to the new person they see in the mirror. They feel different. They become interested in sex.

Self-doubt is constant. They feel pressure to conform and fear ridicule if they don't.

These changes can be bewildering, frightening and even depressing.

Teens can have remarkable insights. But they also surprise us with their lack of good judgment.

Your Teen Needs You.

At the time teenagers are crying out to be treated as adults, they also need a nurturing home, a refuge. And though they deny it passionately, they need structure, limits, lots of help sorting out their lives and most important, love.

In the turbulence of growing up, it is important for us parents to remember (even if our teens seem to forget) that we love each other. In the end, that's what makes the whole struggle worthwhile.

How Well Do You Know Your Kids?

You may say, "My teenager wouldn't do that." Most don't. But even if yours wouldn't, think about the following questions:

- Where is your child right now?
- What are your teen's deepest fears?
- Who is your son or daughter's best friend?
- Do your teen's friends feel welcome in your home?

Remember, a strong relationship with your children is the best way for you to guide them, and to prevent them from becoming a sorry statistic.

Getting Along With Your Teen.

Here are some ideas and techniques you can try to improve your relationship with your teen. If they don't work at first, keep trying. They take practice.

1. Make time for your teen. Find an activity you enjoy doing together and pursue it. If your invitations are declined, keep asking.

2. Listen, really listen. Because parents have so much to do and so little time, we often try to listen while cleaning, washing dishes or fixing the car. Put your chores aside so your teen knows you're really paying attention.

3. Take the long view. Don't treat minor mishaps as major catastrophes. Choose the important issues.

Don't make your home a battleground.

4. Tolerate differences. View your teenager as an individual distinct from you. This doesn't mean you can't state your opinion if you disagree.

5. Respect your teenager's privacy. If a behavior is worrying you, speak up.

6. Let your teens sort things out themselves. Never say that you know how your teen feels. They believe their feelings (so new and personal) are unique. They'll learn otherwise — without your help. And never imply that their feelings don't matter or will change. Because teens live in the present, it doesn't matter that they'll soon feel differently.

7. Don't judge. State facts instead of opinions when you praise or criticize. Stating facts like "Your poem made me smile," or "This report card is all Cs and Ds!" leaves it up to your teen to draw the appropriate conclusions. Teens are sensitive about being judged — positively as well as negatively.

8. Be generous with praise. Praise your child's efforts, not just accomplishments. And don't comment on the person. "You're a great artist" is hard to live up to. "I loved that drawing" is a fact and comes from your heart.

9. Set reasonable limits. Teens need them. Your rules should be consistently applied — and rooted in your deepest beliefs and values.

10. Teach your teen to make sensible decisions and choices by encouraging independence and letting

your teenager make mistakes. Don't step in unless you have to.

How to Make Anger Work.

All parents get furious at their children. We can't help it. But some parents feel bad about being angry and keep quiet. Though it's easy to say things in anger that you don't mean, anger can also spark talks that will help you and your teen get to know each other better.

Some Guidelines.

- When you get mad, don't blame or accuse. Say how you *feel* — annoyed, irritated, upset, etc. — and why. Be specific. Talk facts. Blaming only forces a teen to argue his point, arouses tempers, and kills dialogue.
- Think solution, not victory. Don't try to win arguments.
- Stick to the present incident. Fighting old battles will only aggravate a situation.
- Be careful not to attack your teen's person or character. Say, "I'm furious that you didn't clean up after the mess you made" — *not*, "You're a lazy slob!" Your son or daughter may give up trying to improve.
- If the situation is touchy, put your ideas in a letter. You can say exactly what you mean — and your teen will have time to think it over before

answering.

Signs That Your Child Needs Outside Help.

- Suicidal talk of any kind. A suicidal teen may also give away valued possessions, make a will, talk about death or dying or say his family would be better off without him.
- Recent changes in sleeping or eating habits, thinking patterns, personality, friendships, study habits, activities. A sudden unexplained end to a long depression often precedes a suicide attempt. Major weight loss can be a sign of bulimia or anorexia — dangerous problems.
- Drug or alcohol use. You might notice: irrational or irresponsible behavior, lying, secretiveness, severe mood swings, a sudden increase in accidents. A teen with a problem may have dilated pupils or wear sunglasses indoors, or complain about not sleeping or not feeling well. Valuables may disappear. You may find drug paraphernalia or alcohol containers around the house.
- A recent change in friends who you feel may be involved with drugs or alcohol may indicate that your child is involved or be a sign that your child is having other problems.
- Law-breaking behavior, even if the police and courts aren't involved. You might notice new possessions and money not accounted for.
- Poor self-image. Doubts are normal. But persis-

tently low self-esteem is a problem.
- Serious depression. Listlessness, loneliness, withdrawal, difficulty making friends.
- Rebelliousness to the point of total, continual defiance.
- Problems at school, including class-cutting, absenteeism, a sudden drop in grades.
- Fears or anxieties that interfere with everyday activities.
- Problems between family members that aren't solved by listening and discussing. In fact, family changes such as a death, divorce or remarriage are times when teens often need some outside help.

When to Get Help For Yourself.

- Things aren't going well with your family but you can't figure out why.
- You disagree totally with positions your spouse has taken on issues concerning your teen and the two of you can't find a compromise.
- You have trouble holding a job.
- You are abusing drugs or alcohol.
- You get violent with your teenager and can't control yourself.
- Your spouse gets violent with you or your child.

What to Do If Your Teen Runs Away.

Most kids who run away return within 48 hours. Those who stay away can find themselves in many dangerous situations. So do everything you can to bring your child home.

- Keep a notebook recording steps you've taken and dates.
- Check in with: neighbors, relatives, and your teen's friends, teachers, employer or co-workers.
- Contact local hangouts and hospitals.
- Call the police. Have an officer come to your house to take a report and pick up recent photos, dental records and fingerprints if available. Get his name; badge number and phone number; the police report number; and the name of the officer who will follow up.
- Make sure the police lists your teen in the National Crime Information Center (NCIC) to the state clearinghouse on missing children, if there is one in your state.
- Contact the National Center for Missing and Exploited Children for help with law enforcement officials — 1-800-843-5678.
- Call the Covenant House NINELINE for support and to check for messages. Leave a message. Also check with any local runaway hotlines.
- Contact runaway shelters locally and in nearby states.
- Make posters with photos of your teen, listing: age, height, weight, hair and eye color, complexion, physical characteristics (such as scars, birthmarks, braces or pierced ears), circumstances of disappearance, your phone number and police con-

tacts. Distribute these to truck stops, youth-oriented businesses, hospitals, law-enforcement agencies.

- Be prepared for the first conversation with your teen. Whether in person or by phone, show concern, not anger. Say, "I love you."

- Prepare to quickly begin resolving the problems which caused your child to leave home. When your child returns home, emotions are likely to run high. Someone outside your family can help you all deal with these emotions. You may find that planned time for your teen in a temporary residence or shelter is necessary while you are resolving problems. So get outside help from a trained counselor.

Need expert advice or support?

Call our NINELINE counselors at 1-800-999-9999.

We'll put you in touch with people who can help you right in your hometown.

1-800-999-9999

This call is free.

Covenant House
346 West 17th Street
New York, NY 10011-5002

Covenant House Florida
733 Breakers Avenue
Fort Lauderdale, FL 33304-4196

Covenant House New Orleans
611 North Rampart Street
New Orleans, LA 70112-3540

Covenant House Alaska
609 F Street
Anchorage, AK 99501-3596

Covenant House California
1325 N. Western Avenue
Hollywood, CA 90027-5611

Covenant House Texas
1111 Lovett Boulevard
Houston, TX 77006-3898

Covenant House Donor Assistance Line: 1-800-388-3888

"I bound myself oath, I made a covenant with you ... and you became mine."   **Ezekiel 16:8**

The only way to stop the pain and degradation of street children is to get more people involved in solutions to the devastating problems they face every night of their lives.

After you read this book, please pass it along to a friend. If you would like more copies, just fill out this coupon and return it to us in the envelope provided. And know that because you took the time to care, a kid won't have to sell himself to survive tonight.

Please send me _____ **copies of** *God Isn't Done With Me Yet....* **To help defray the cost of sending you these books, we request a minimum donation of $5 per book.**

Name _____

Address _____

City _____ **State** _____ **Zip** _____

Please make your check payable to Covenant House.
Your gift is tax deductible.

Many people like to charge their gift. If you would like to, please fill out the information below:

I prefer to charge my: _____ **MasterCard** _____ **Visa**

Account # _____

Amount _____ **Exp. Date** _____

Signature _____

Mail to: **Covenant House**
                   JAF Box 2973
                   New York, NY 10116-2973

COUPON

Or, call 1-800-388-3888 to charge your gift on your MasterCard® or Visa® or to get more information.

> *"I bound myself oath, I made a covenant with you ... and you became mine."*
>
> *Ezekiel 16:8*

Covenant House depends almost entirely on gifts from friends like you to help 35,000 homeless and runaway children every year. We provide food, clothing, shelter, medical attention, educational and vocational training, and counseling to kids with no place to go for help. Please help if you can.

YES! I want to help the kids at Covenant House.
Here is my gift of: ☐ $10 ☐ $20 ☐ $25 ☐ Other

Name _____

Address _____

City _____ **State** _____ **Zip** _____
Please make your check payable to Covenant House.
Your gift is tax deductible.

Many people like to charge their gift. If you would like to, please fill out the information below:

I prefer to charge my: _____ MasterCard _____ Visa

Account # _____

Amount _____ **Exp. Date** _____

Signature _____

Mail to: **Covenant House**
JAF Box 2973
New York, NY 10116-2973

COUPON

Or, call 1-800-388-3888 to charge your gift.

Copies of our financial and operating reports have been filed with the state and are available on request. To obtain one, simply write: New York State Department of State, Charities Registration Section, 162 Washington Avenue, Albany, NY 12231 or Covenant House, JAF Box 2973, New York, NY 10116-2973.

West Virginia residents may obtain a summary of the registration and financial documents from the Secretary of State, State Capitol, Charleston, WV 25305. Registration does not imply endorsement.